AF413243

To Sheila Starr
the Halloween OG

And to Annie
for all the love and light
you have brought to my life

Ghosty House: A True Story
Copyright © 2024 by Veronica A. Rangel

All rights reserved. No part of this book may be used or reproduced in any manner whatsoever without written permission except in the case of brief quotations embodied in critical articles or reviews.

Thank you for buying an authorized edition of this book and for complying with copyright laws by not reproducing, scanning or distributing any part of it in any form without permission. You are supporting writers and artists and their hard work by doing this.

For information contact:
Veronica A. Rangel at www.veronicaarangel.com

Written by Sheila Starr Schumaker and illustrated by Veronica A. Rangel

ISBN: 979-8-3304-3926-3

Library of Congress Cataloging-in-Publication Data is available
Printed in the United States of America
10 9 8 7 6 5 4 3 2 1
First Edition: October 2024

GHOSTY HOUSE

A True Story

written by **Sheila Starr Schumaker**

illustrated by **Veronica A. Rangel**

The summer was quickly coming to an end. Annie could hardly wait until the weather turned cooler. She could hardly wait until the leaves began to change colors and start their descent off the trees. A curious spider had attached himself onto a crimson leaf just as the north wind flipped and tossed it, sailing it toward the earth below. That morning, the dawn had finally cradled in its blanket of morning dew and signaled the season of fall to begin and welcome Annie's favorite holiday. HALLOWEEN! A time when Annie could be anything she ever wanted to be.

ctob
Sunday
Monday
Tuesday
Wednesday
Thursday
1
2
3
4
5
8
9
10
15
16
17
18
20
22
23
24
25
26
27
29
30
31

One year, she was a princess and yet another time an astronaut. But this year, she was going to be a pirate. This year, she was going to the neighborhood house around the corner that turned itself into the best ghosty house of all. She counted the days and she counted the nights until at long last the magical night arrived.

Annie piled up all her pirate stuff. It was time to get ready. She got her pirate hat. She got her pirate sword. She got her pirate vest and eye patch. The patch was to put over her one eye.

The moon was starting its steep climb into the cold night sky. Long dark shadows slipped off the trees and crept like gnarled fingers snaking their way along the side walks and streets.

The heavens were getting ready for the spookiest night of the year. And, as the clouds rolled furiously across the deep blue sky, you could see a witch sailing on behind the moon.

Annie was a great pirate and ready for a great pirate adventure. She got her flashlight and empty bucket for her holiday treats and walked out into the Halloween night. She walked down to the corner. The curious spider decided to go with her.

She could smell the air. It was crisp autumn air. A smell that only comes at that time of year. A smell from burning leaves and pine logs that had etched its way into her memory. As she turned the corner, she heard it - the sounds. The sounds of Halloween.

They were coming from the **GHOSTY HOUSE**

The sounds of cats screaming, chains clanking, doors creaking and bells tolling filled the air. They sent chills down Annie's spine and made her wish she had never ventured out. "Great Halloween sounds." she thought as she got closer to the house. Fog started rolling over her head. "I must be getting closer to the graveyard,"

she thought again. Suddenly, it was there. Towering over her head were the giant gates of the haunted graveyard. Tombstones of all kinds were everywhere. Horrible, wonderful Halloween ghosts were roaming through this ghastly place. Annie slipped through the gates and wondered to herself, "what's going to happen now?"

Esmerlda and Broomhilda, two wart-riddled witches, were brewing candy in a cauldron so huge, it was as big as Annie herself.

Fire leaped from the bottom of the monster pot and steam billowed out of the top. Annie saw other children reaching into the cauldron for their candy. Annie couldn't do it. Annie was too scared. But, Annie loved being scared.

Annie then came upon a laboratory
where Doctor Frankenstein was
operating on the monster.

The doctor had just finished sewing on the monster's head. Annie could hardly watch. This really scared Annie. But, Annie loved being scared.

RIP
Annie hit her foot against something: "Good grief, it's a coffin," Annie squealed. It was Dracula's coffin.

At that very moment, he began to sit straight up.
Dracula reached his cold, clammy hand out to Annie.
Annie couldn't extend her hand out to help. Annie
was so scared. But, Annie loved being scared.

All of a sudden, she heard a terrible noise. The noise was the sound of a chain saw. An ugly zombie was chasing after Annie. She heard the chain saw buzzing, the witches cackling, Dracula screaming and Dr. Frankenstein's monster groaning.

She ran faster than she had ever run before. Annie was shaking scared. But, Annie loved being scared.

She ran and ran until she was in front of her own house, safe again. Annie knew she was in no danger. The not-so-curious spider was still clutching onto her hat and thankful he hadn't fallen off. She knew it was all make believe or was it? "One thing," she thought, "I never did get my candy from the giant cauldron."

The next day, after Annie had breakfast, she got dressed quickly and went back to the Ghosty House. It was all gone. The graveyard, the tombstones, the laboratory,

the monster – they were all gone. The coffin with Dracula
was also gone. The chain saw had even disappeared.
The only thing left was the monstrous pot.

A lady was standing by it and called to
Annie, "Did you get your Halloween candy
last night?" "No!" replied Annie. "Then come
over here and get some," she shrilled. Annie
slowly walked up to the cauldron and to her
surprise, she was given a handful of candies.

"Did you enjoy being scared last night even though everything was make believe?," asked the woman. "OH YES! I loved being scared," said Annie. "You know, you can never be sure of what is real and what is not. Can you?," said the lady mysteriously. With a wink of her eye and a twist of her wrist, she turned herself into an ugly old witch with a green wart on her nose. Annie shrieked in horror and was scared all over again. But Annie loved being scared.

Forty five years ago, my mom, Sheila Starr, with a group of her creative friends and her technically-savvy husband, created one of the very first home haunts – way before Halloween became the huge holiday we celebrate today. Everything was created by hand back then, because it just wasn't available to buy.

For 15 years, Starr's "Ghosty House" grew every year – delighting its visitors with a haunted, tombstone-filled graveyard and 15 minute shows of Doctor Frankenstein experimenting on his monster in an all-too-real scientific lab. Sounds of cats would scream, chains clanked, and doors creaked while witches gave out candy out of a monstrous cauldron, Dracula rose from his coffin, and a chainsaw-wielding zombie would creep out of the ever present fog, ready to scare.

Eventually, my mom got older and gates went up in her community, so she sunsetted her Ghosty House experience, although remnants remained, like her monstrous cauldron in her front lawn, which was actually a 150 year old Wells Fargo gold smelt.

Toward the end of its run, my mom wrote a children's book about her Ghosty House, telling the story of a little girl who visits the spookiest house in her neighborhood on Halloween night. Since I was a graphic designer, she asked me to illustrate it. We worked out a storyboard and mockup, and I illustrated a few of the spreads. Then we presented it to every publisher we could find, but it wasn't "discovered" in the mountain of manuscripts they received daily.

We put our dreams of publishing Ghosty House aside, and life went on. The years went by, and once in a while, the mockup of Ghosty House would resurface. I would read it and smile, and remember how much fun those days were – creating an experience that everyone could enjoy, with a lot of creativity and little bit of scary.

My mom passed away 7 years ago, and recently, the Ghosty House mockup turned up again, but this time, I saw it with fresh eyes. I now have three grown up children, the third being a curly haired girl named Annie who loved her grandmother and got to witness the beautiful, creative spark in the universe that was my mom. Annie would not be born for 15 years after we created the mockup, but when I saw it again, all I saw was my daughter, Annie, in the pages of my mom's story – same curly hair, same spunky attitude.

I realized that I could now make the dream of publishing my mom's book a reality, thanks to modern technology. Publishing Ghosty House and my mom's legacy has come full circle, and it means the world to me. Enjoy!

Veronica A. Rangel

www.ingramcontent.com/pod-product-compliance
Lightning Source LLC
Chambersburg PA
CBRC090518160726
48196CB00090B/737